SCALE

THEN

SELL

**The Blueprint For Unlocking
What The 1% Know About Growth**

MICHAEL BYARS

COPYRIGHT 2021 BY MICHAEL BYARS

ALL RIGHTS RESERVED

NO PART OF THIS PUBLICATION MAY BE REPLICATED, DUPLICATED OR REPUBLISHED WITHOUT THE WRITTEN PERMISSION OF MICHAEL BYARS

ISBN: 9798740994918

Imprint: Independently published

TABLE OF CONTENTS

It's Cause and Effect 1
"How am I going to scale this business!?" 8
100% of a Grape or 50% of a Watermelon? 11
Transferring Scale to Others 15
PART ONE: YOUR VISION 22
Winners Have Vision 23
The Ultimate Insurance 29
Connect with Your Purpose 32
My Initial Spark 35
PART TWO: YOUR WORK ETHIC AND YOUR VALUES 39
Tell the Truth 40
Be a Worker 42
Be a Collaborator 45
Be a Leader 47
Create an All-Star Team 52
Commit to Excellence 59
Always Sell 61
Set Your Planning Time 62
PART THREE: YOUR SYSTEMS 65
Know what you want, then who can do it 68
Roles and Results 70
Never Delegate Your Courage 75
Never Delegate Your Learning Curve 76
Just Do It 77
CONCLUSION 81
About the Author 84

It's Cause and Effect

If you grow your company with the intention that you're going to sell it at some point, you will build a *better company*.

Whether you do in fact sell it remains optional.

But your intention affects the actions you take, and therefore your results: your revenue, profit, time with family, how satisfied you and your team are, and the amount of positive change you can create in the marketplace.

With some entrepreneurs, they don't want to sell their business once they start scaling it. They're finally having fun again, and loving the growth. And I know exactly what that feels like because I've experienced it…

How I Solved The "One-Man Company" Trap and Became a "Master of Scale"

At a young age, I saw the cause-and-effect relationship between action and results.

In South Carolina, there are a lot of farms.

While sitting in the back seat of my parents' car, I watched the farmland pass by the window.

I noticed the farmers tilling the soil in the spring.

They cared for their fields in the summer.

They harvested their take in autumn.

Then, those farmers did it all over again the following spring.

As I reflect on my business career, I appreciate those honest and hardworking people. They inspire me just as much as the business icons we all read about.

They taught me something about cause and effect:

If you plant a seed in good soil, water it, and give it sunlight: the seed will grow and provide you with the fruits of your labor.

If you remove any one of those elements: nothing happens.

Take away the water and the seed will dry up and die.

Take away the sunlight: it rots.

Take away the soil: the birds eat it or it blows away with the wind.

Give that seed all three elements consistently over time and the plant will almost always grow strong and provide you with the end result you desire.

The same principle applies to business.

Give your business the right fuel in the proper order consistently over time and your business will grow.

It baffles me how so few individuals – sincere people, really good people – seem to misconceive "success" as if it's magic. The secret is: there is no magic!

It's a process.

It's mathematics.

It's the *consequence* of a series of actions.

When you define what you want to turn your business into, keep that vision in your mind, architect systems and processes into your business for long-term growth: your business will provide you with the resources and the lifestyle you desire.

One night you'll go to sleep.

You'll wake up the next morning, and realize you have arrived where you have always wanted to be.

You will have surpassed your original financial goals.

You've been able to take time with your family and enjoy some good times.

You've been able to buy yourself nicer things too.

Perhaps you've even moved into a better home!

You've been able to support causes that are important to you. You finally created the business you once imagined for yourself, and it supports you like the foundation of your new home.

That also results in a new feeling. You feel more self-worth, dignity, and personal satisfaction.

Why have so many people forgotten how to apply the natural laws of growth to their business?

It seems like most folks don't think about long-term commitments.

They want quick wins, fast hacks, and instant gains.

They act as if a seed could instantly *pop!* into an apple tree.

They secretly wish business and entrepreneurship could be *easy*.

Imagine, what would happen instead if the majority asked for better *skills* to thrive through difficult or challenging situations?

Or maybe more courage to implement systems they know have worked for others?

Imagine, if that were the headline.

Yet, it's not.

It's the *hack*.

So, what's the consequence?

For the majority of people who start a business, it's one of two things.

They either go broke. Give up. Close shop.

Or, they grow their company to a certain level, get stuck in a rut, and can't scale beyond that point.

In other words, they've created a job for themselves they are handcuffed to at all times.

They're trapped.

They're spinning out of control on their personal hamster wheel.

And since their business orbits around them, and their personal labor (or a very small team), it's not a very valuable business to buy either.

I was in the second camp.

I didn't realize at the time how to properly scale my business.

Even though I've never given up and closed my doors, I know what it's like to want to.

I understand how it feels to be *The One-Man Company:* the hamster on the wheel.

I've been the receptionist at eight AM…

The head salesperson by nine…

The marketing director and accountant around noon…

The CEO in the afternoon (if I was lucky.) …

… and finally: the janitor before leaving at nine PM.

My business felt like a tornado of chaos.

That affected my mindset in my personal life.

There were no clear boundaries between work and home.

The money was good. I was earning 100% of the profit of the business I brought in. Yet, even though I was earning a good living, I was losing a connection to my personal life.

I was not giving my family the attention they deserved.

I was constantly stressed out.

There were moments I'd get home, and my son was telling me about his day.

He was happy as could be, trying to talk to me about something important to him.

Yet, nothing was getting through to me.

I imagine I was probably just sitting there, staring into space, thinking about whether or not I had responded to an email.

Kids pick up on that stuff: when you're there, but not *there.* Thinking of not being present with my little boy trying to connect with me really hurts. Time with family is one of the most important things in life. They are number one. I hope you share that same value.

What's the point of earning more money if you can't use it to spend more time with your family?

Those moments added up and the feeling compounded.

I was spending more time at work and less time with my family. Even when I was there, I wasn't present.

Plus: my extra efforts were not paying off!

That's one of the most frustrating experiences: working harder in your business and not experiencing any payoff or measurable progress. It's like shackles.

My effort wasn't moving the bottom line.

I felt aggravated and restless.

It was not working.

At some point, that pain reached a new threshold, I couldn't tolerate it anymore, I remember almost screaming out loud in my office…

"How am I going to scale this business!?"

After asking myself that question too many times to count, the most logical first step was to invest in my education.

So, I hit the business books hard.

I looked for ideas and systems I could apply to my *One-Man Company*.

It was an I.T. and technical support business.

I read books by Robert Kiyosaki, Michael Gerber, Tony Robbins, Steven Covey, Warren Buffet, and Peter Drucker (to name a few).

I became a student of systems, delegation, and leadership.

I sought the help of a business coach I admired.

I filled my mind with as much wisdom as I could.

I had a burning desire; an obsession to create growth.

The question changed, too:

"How can I scale this business, *without me "doing" it?*"

Also:

"How would I build this if I wanted to sell it at some point?"

Piece by piece, while always maintaining my focus on long-term growth, I developed and implemented new systems to buy back my time and scale my business.

I refined my marketing and sales process. (I figured that'd be a good place to start because that's where all the revenue starts).

Then, I created systems for the fulfilment of our services.

Delivering our service became something we could replicate over and over, meeting the demand as it came.

That extended the lifetime value of each of our clients, thus making the company more sustainable over the long-term, and also more valuable if someone were to buy it.

Then, we did the same for our follow-up processes. When projects were complete, what then? How do we offer more value to our customers and get them to refer us?

I went through our business top to bottom.

It was no longer just me: it was *we,* and our team worked together to systematize everything from advertising to accounting.

If we didn't know how to automate a process, we hired someone skilled in that area to help us.

We tested and retested approaches for finding and hiring great technicians (the doers).

We also became efficient at working with managers and forming an *inner circle* of executive staff.

Delegation became a science.

Automation became a habit.

Processes became law.

And, the results were MASSIVE.

It was "wide open" both the profit the company was able to achieve, my personal income, as well as the time and energy I was able to gain back.

To give you an idea of verifiable results, here's what it looked like…

100% of a Grape or 50% of a Watermelon?

When I first started my tech support company, I owned *all* of that small business.

That's what I call "owning 100% of a grape."

What that looked like is this: I was earning $146K annually, and I kept all the profit.

That's not bad at all, still in the top 5% of income-earners.

Yet, as I mentioned my time and energy were spent.

There was no possible way I could scale it beyond that point.

The market potential in that industry was thousands of times multiples greater than what I could possibly tackle on my own (Imagine looking beyond the grape at giant watermelon).

That brought up an important question I had to ask myself:

"Would you rather own 100% of this grape, or 50% of that big watermelon?"

Do you want *all* of a small tart, or *part* of a large pie?

In terms of profit, quality of time, and satisfaction, the answer was clear: I'd rather own part of the watermelon (and a nice chunk of pie too!).

Let me prove why that mindset is so important.

One year after implementing the processes I mentioned above, my $146K "grape" business transformed into a $896K "watermelon."

That's 6.15x growth.

The year after that, we grew to $2.1 million.

The next year, I invested in a parallel business, so we earned $1.1 million. Then, the next year: $2.8 million.

Also, that was net profit.

Our gross revenues were much higher.

That's only one company. As a result of these systems, not only were we able to scale *it*, we then applied the same principles to our real estate investing business, as well as other people's companies (which I'll get to in a moment).

The increased income was great. There was a certain pride in helping other families support themselves too through employment. Yet, as I mentioned before, quality time with family is *most* important. Being able to take more time with my wife and son was the most satisfying part of the systems we integrated.

Through the power of teamwork, systems, and technology, we transformed my *One-Man Company* into an organization where we maximize each person's skills.

Our employees are doing what they are great at and love most, and I finally became the entrepreneur I had envisioned.

Yet, the story doesn't end there.

Yes, our team transformed into an "self-managing" organization.

That's great, and the time with family was wonderful too.

But then, everything changed in a *bigger way.*

Other business owners started taking notice.

The people in my network (and even vendors we were working with) started asking all sorts of questions about how we were growing.

Since I'm always willing to help fellow entrepreneurs who are stuck at some sort of a road-block in their career, I felt honored for the opportunity to share some of the knowledge I had gained.

It was rewarding: discovering the challenges these business people had, and offering suggestions on how to solve them.

I found myself asking these people:

"What's working for you now?"

"Where do you want to take this company?"

"What are your sticking points?"

"What actions are you taking to overcome them now?"

Probably 95% of these entrepreneurs had the same problem I once had: their business leveled off at a plateau, and they could not scale beyond that point no matter how hard they tried.

I witnessed case after case of that awful hamster wheel of a one-man show, turning infinitely, spinning these good people around.

They were in the same position I was in only five years before. Once I got clarity about their situation, I offered suggestions based on my experiences. Some of those owners went on to create growth in their companies as well.

But something *even more surprising* started happening!

Transferring Scale to Others

Some of the business owners were looking for partnerships, more capital, or infrastructure to help grow their business. So we started investing in other companies.

We own some commercial real estate and one of the tenants is a CBD company. I spoke to my advisory council about that industry and whether it was a safe long-term play.

We did our due diligence, felt good about the numbers, and made an investment in their company. Now we're scaling the business. At the time of writing this, it has the largest footprint on the East Coast of the United States, with a CBD extraction facility of 92,000 square feet.

Another example is our real estate holding company. I was travelling a lot, and wanted to invest in some property. That way, if something were to happen to me (knock on wood), then my family would be covered.

As I increased the total number of doors we owned, the complexity grew. So, I applied the same principles I learned in the tech support business and we developed a new property management company. That action enabled us to scale our real estate portfolio by more than ten times. We went from fifteen residential doors to one-hundred sixty-five, and ten commercial buildings. But not only that. We turned it into its own profit center by offering the service to other investors. Now it's a self-managing and profitable company that offers tons of value to the marketplace.

More grapes into watermelons.

Making more juice for everyone.

It's all in the power of process, delegation, and systems.

Another recent and surprising one…

I'm a partner in a bakery! (Of all things).

I would have had no clue about how to invest in a business like that, and ordinarily would have passed up on the opportunity.

Yet, through the experience of working in the other industries I mentioned, we had a framework for maximizing the market potential of other service-related businesses.

The bakery's numbers made sense. We went for it.

I used the same framework in a mulching business.

Later, also an Amazon-store management company.

In the Amazon business we took revenues from $3 Million to $70 million in less than six months. That's as a direct result of introducing new systems and support into our partner's small business.

Again: grapes into watermelons.

As you can probably understand: each of these company's deliverables (the products and services they fulfil) and benefits to the end client are different from one another.

The CBD company has a different product than the real estate company.

The real estate company knows nothing about making bread.

The baker knows nothing about how to scale an Amazon store.

One is local. The other is e-commerce.

One offers a product. The other offers a service.

They all have unique logistics and systems and sales cycles.

Question: why do you think we've been able to grow and scale such *different* business models, and how could you do the same? The answer is in the three-part structure of this book.

It's the *vision* you have for yourself and your business, the *work ethic* you demonstrate on an ongoing basis (which impacts both your actions and your employee's and partners), and the *systems* you incorporate in your business to maximize your leverage.

Understand this: your product or service deliverables are almost certainly different than the ones I mentioned above.

Your deliverable may not be tech support, CBD oils, real estate, tasty cookies, mulching equipment, or Amazon products like the business I'm invested in.

It does not matter that you're in a different industry.

That is not the important part.

You are selling something to someone. If you are the only person doing it (or you have a very small team with inefficient systems) then you're limited to that twenty-four-hour clock, and your own two hands. The majority of businesspeople who read this book have a "watermelon" opportunity in their market. But are only taking a grape's worth of value from it. Plus, they're killing themselves in the process by draining their time pressing the buttons and pulling the levers themselves.

That's why I wrote this book. I understand what it's like, struggling to grow a company, and finally break through the ceiling. The bottom line is that I want to share how to grow more hands and get more time (metaphorically speaking).

At some point, if you'd like to sell your company for many multiples more than what you could now, then that's an option. That's actually the premise of *Scale Then Sell:* instead of staying on the hamster wheel (or worse, closing your doors and letting your business go) you consciously scale it, increase its value and make it more appealing to an investor.

The other option is to continue growing your company with the increased satisfaction and fulfilment you get from only doing the things you're superior at because you have systems in place to do your best work.

What you're going to get from the following chapters is not *everything* you need to know about growing your company. I chose, instead, to focus on three of my core principles for scaling a business, not tactics.

In part one we'll explore entrepreneurial *vision,* what it means to be a visionary, and how to cultivate your vision for long-term growth.

Then, in part two we'll talk about the type of *work ethic and values* you need if you want to grow as an entrepreneur and businessperson. The qualities I'll share with you in part two are exactly what I look for in the business owners we partner with, invest in, and mentor. If you have the qualities I outline, not only can I guarantee you will succeed in business, you'll also likely be a good fit to work in partnership, or to get involved in the *Scale-Then-Sell* universe. My partners and I put together all sorts of training for business owners like you, and we'd be happy to share our "secrets" for free (see link below).

Lastly, in part three we'll talk about how to (literally) buy back your time and energy. Part three is all about your *systems.* These insights are centered around working on your business, and not *in* it.

Sincerely,

Michael

PART ONE: YOUR VISION

WANT TO MASTER THE SCALE-THEN-SELL SYSTEM?

Check Out the Complimentary

Scale-Then-Sell Resources at:

www.ScaleThenSell.com/Book

Winners Have Vision

If you walk up to a hundred people on the street, and ask them, "What do you want to accomplish in the next year, specifically?" You'd be amazed at how many people cannot give you an answer.

Walk from that street into a business networking event. The results aren't much different. The bottom line is this: Most people do not know what they want, and because of this, their business follows suit.

Serial winners, on the other hand, set goals for themselves. This is true in any category, whether it's business, sports, entertainment: any career or pursuit where high achievers excel.

They know exactly what they want.

They make a plan to accomplish it.

They follow that plan over the long term, until they win.

When they experience a setback, they do not think of it as a failure. They are so connected to their vision that, no matter what happens externally, those serial winners use the circumstances as opportunities to pivot, shift, and adapt.

In the book *Psycho Cybernetics,* Dr. Maxwell Maltz writes "We act or fail to act, not because of 'will,' as is so commonly believed, but because of imagination."

Steve Jobs understood this. All great leaders do. His vision led Apple through three decades in an industry where change is the only constant.

He once said, "If you are working on something exciting that you really care about, you don't have to be pushed. The vision pulls you."

With vision, you can persevere through almost any challenge.

How do you respond when an important client shops around and starts doing business with another company?

What about when an employee jumps ship, or drops the ball on a big project?

What about when a vendor doesn't deliver, or partner does something unethical, or a virus outbreak completely disintegrates your marketing strategy or even your whole business?

On that last note, when I wrote the first draft of this book, COVID-19 had shut down the country.

By September 2020, the pandemic had already permanently closed 100,00 businesses across the country.

I watched how people responded.

Some of them got out there and worked harder than ever; adapting to the ever-changing world, and economy.

Those are my type of people.

They're the people who turn the most complex circumstances into opportunities.

They are pulled forward by their vision.

Napoleon Hill shared in *Think and Grow Rich:* "Every adversity carries with it the seed of an equal or greater opportunity."

The people I mention are the ones who water those seeds and make them real.

Other people, on the opposite side of the professional spectrum, were camped out at home, waiting on their "stimulus check" to save the day.

When all the shut downs started, one of my businesses went from a few million-dollars in revenue to *nothing.*

Imagine that happening: over $50,000 in monthly payroll to cover, and within a one-week period of time, no revenue coming in. It was a complete disruption to our lives, *everyone's life.*

It shook the lives of my team, and they immediately looked to me for leadership. I took a massive hit to my monthly income, and that scared me. But I had to pull it together and readjust.

At that point, I had my own family to consider, plus all sixty of my employee's families to worry about too – at least 180 people, almost half a Boeing 747, all who were relying on my leadership to bring my A+ game.

I had to step up, and make something happen.

Did I sit at home and wait on my stimulus check to arrive?

Definitely not.

I pivoted so fast; it made my head spin.

I became my own stimulus check.

I went out there and made something out of nothing.

I started a brand-new business in those crazy times.

That's what true entrepreneurs do: double down.

They go harder.

They meet the resistance head on and do not pull punches.

In February of 2020 this new business venture was making no money. In April of 2020 it made over $40,000, and in May of 2020 we created over $60,000 worth of jobs on the schedule.

That growth and ability to scale is dependent on my team, our work ethic, and willingness to adapt. It is also shaped by an openness to take a chance.

It's all about being willing to make the intelligent and informed choice.

What's the most logical thing to do right now?

Weigh out your options, see which one makes the most sense, and execute.

If it doesn't work: readjust.

That was what needed to happen when the tech support business dropped, and I entered the mulching business.

That was a new arena for me. But I spotted an opportunity. All the competitors were advertising price. You know that's the kiss of death because some other guy can come in and underbid you.

We saw the opportunity to position the value, not price.

So, we went for it.

We invested in two rigs, priced at a quarter million dollars apiece, doubled down on the advertising, and went wide open with it.

I took a chance, and that's what life is all about.

At the end of the day, it's also what got me where I am.

I may have won some and lost others.

But every experience is a chance to learn. Each experience compounds into a more calculated risk the next time I decide to place my bet on a business.

You will never hit the ball if you don't swing. You need to have the courage to get out there and keep taking shots. You've probably heard it a hundred times, but I'll quote Wayne Gretzky: "You miss 100% of the shots you don't take."

You can become your own stimulus check!

But do you want it bad enough?

Unexpected circumstances happen in life.

They can leave you feeling like you just took a sucker punch to the gut.

As an entrepreneur, your greatest asset is maintaining your confidence and weathering any potential storm you experience.

It's also hustling like crazy when circumstances are working in your favor and you have an advantage.

The Ultimate Insurance

How do you overcome adversity when times are hard, and maximize opportunities when circumstances are running in your favor?

The answer, first and foremost, is your *personal vision*.

Your personal vision is the secret of staying power.

It's the ultimate insurance plan.

It makes you stand your ground when chaos is happening all around you.

It makes you grind like a madman when the wind dies down.

Your personal vision is the most critical factor to your long-term success in business.

One of my favorite examples of a rock-solid personal vision is Ray Kroc.

He turned McDonald's into one of the most successful franchises in history.

When he started McDonald's, Kroc was fifty-two years old.

He was missing his gallbladder and most of his thyroid.

He suffered from diabetes and arthritis too.

Kroc had every excuse to start slowing down.

Yet, as he put it: "You're either green and growing, or ripe and rotting."

So, he went for it at fifty-two.

Most people his age, in his condition, had probably given up on their lives long before. Instead, Ray Kroc envisioned something in his mind, and he pursued it consistently until it became a reality.

He showed up to work at 7:30 AM to 5:30 PM as a paper cup salesman, took a two-hour break, and then got back at it from 8 PM to 2 AM as a piano man for a Chicago Radio station.

Paper cups by day, piano by night.

He took the profits he earned, and saved them long enough to purchase the rights to a milkshake machine.

He traveled the country for seventeen years, selling those milkshake machines to restaurant owners.

Seventeen years!

His hustle paid off the day he visited the McDonald brothers' California burger restaurant.

Ray saw their small burger business turning into a global empire.

He held that vision in his mind.

In 1961, he bought the McDonald brothers' franchise.

Within a short few years, he had sold billions of burgers and opened 500 franchise stores.

Vision and tenacity cannot be bought.

You may not like McDonald's.

No problem.

Still, the fact remains: their systematic approach to growing a world-wide company revolutionized the way businesses run in America.

That model – the replicable, scalable, franchise prototype – will be studied in business colleges and universities for generations to come.

That all began with Ray Kroc's *personal vision*.

In his own words: "That night in my motel room I did a lot of heavy thinking about what I'd seen during the day. Visions of McDonald's restaurants dotting crossroads all over the country paraded through my brain."

Connect with Your Purpose

Consider the following questions.

You can write the answers down if you want to take it to the next level.

But, please take a moment and think about how you'd answer these questions at this point in your journey.

- Do you remember what made you start your business in the first place? What was it?

- Do you recall that first spark of passion to create your own business?
- What's your unique contribution to the world?
- What is the future vision you hold for yourself?
- What do you want to spend your time doing?
- What experiences do you want to create?
- What roles are going to satisfy and fulfil you most?

For some people, they're like me: they grew up not having much and wanted a better life for themselves.

They never knew what it was like to travel, for instance, and that was the thing that gave them that initial spark of motivation.

For others, the thought of finally being recognized, contributing to their community – those are the feelings that initiated their entrepreneurial careers.

Whatever your motivation: commit to keep refueling that passion, and making it burn stronger.

You will need it.

When the going gets rough, when you're experiencing setbacks, and the onlookers (regular civilians with employee mentalities) advise you to give up, and be reasonable, and "get a job," it's vitally important to maintain your inner conviction that what you're doing is important to you.

Stay connected with your personal motivation, your mission, and your reasons for wanting to pursue the entrepreneurial path.

That purpose will keep you strong and focused and moving forward whenever you reach a dead end, take a tough break, or need to reinvent your business model and adjust to changes.

When you identify your personal *why*, you can rely on yourself to pick yourself back up and keep going toward your mark.

In the words of the legendary coach and motivational speaker Zig Ziglar, "The way you see life will largely determine what you get out of it."

Also, when you're leading people, whether it's your team or clients, they are picking up on the unconscious signals you send them.

Someone with no vision may be able to get by when business is going well.

Yet, they'll never innovate anything transformational.

They'll also flake off and blow away with the wind when an economic storm comes.

Only the people with vision lead others.

They are a rock in uncertain times.

They are the foundation.

They are the source of reassurance people seek so desperately.

If you want to be that rock, you must have a clear idea of what you want.

Connect with your personal vision.

My Initial Spark

Before we get into the next section, I'd like to tell you a quick story about some initial experiences as a child that helped shape my vision as an entrepreneur. It may be instructive as a case-study. However, I'm suggesting as you read this to consider your earliest experiences and memories, and ask yourself how you may turn those into motivation.

We didn't have much growing up.

My parents worked hard to provide for our family.

They did the best they could.

As a kid I remember feeling like I was in heaven, savoring every bite of a McDonald's hamburger, thinking to myself, "I cannot believe this is actually happening right now!"

Meaning, it was a real treat for my parents to take us out for a dinner like that.

Those outings rarely happened.

When they did, it was something special to be grateful for.

As a land surveyor, my father was skilled at math.

He could do complicated math calculations in his head.

He also could envision what a piece of land could become.

I found it fascinating how a construction company could turn a field of grass and dirt into a retail outlet, apartment complex, or whatever.

How did they do that?

It seemed so complicated; too many moving parts.

It baffled my mind as a child.

As time went on, through enough conversations with my father, I realized real estate is pure logic. The buildings stand on a foundation of math.

So do the investor's profits and cash-flow.

My mother was a teacher.

She compelled me to spend a lot of time in the library.

My nose was always stuck between the pages of a book.

She passed down her curiosity for life.

I was constantly learning, thinking, and imagining.

She taught me how books are the secret to discovering new parts of the world, without needing to buy a plane ticket to go there.

National Geographic was one of the magazines that sparked my interest in far-away places.

My mind was captivated by their different lifestyles, clothing, sounds, and languages.

I read about the foods and my mouth salivated, thinking about what it would be like to travel the world one day.

Then, I'd come out of my trance, back to reality, back to South Carolina where a plane ticket and travel were out of the question.

That was my initial spark to become an entrepreneur: I wanted to travel the world and experience the destinations I had read about as a child. To do that, I knew I would need to apply the creativity my mother had taught me, as well as my father's logic, and both of their *work ethic.*

This leads me to one of the most important factors that will determine your success as an entrepreneur…

PART TWO: YOUR WORK ETHIC AND YOUR VALUES

> **WANT TO MASTER THE SCALE-THEN-SELL SYSTEM?**
> Check Out the Complimentary Scale-Then-Sell Resources at:
> www.ScaleThenSell.com/Book

You have vision.

Now it's time to make it real.

We make our vision real through our work ethic and values.

In this section I'll outline a few qualities I've noticed in every high-performing entrepreneur who turns companies into legacies.

Tell the Truth

Social media has created a whole new cloud of smoke and mirrors. People position themselves as if they're an expert, without having paid their dues. The barrier to entry is so low that it's hard to tell who's legitimate, and who is not full of it.

I know you've seen it too: someone establishes a "personal brand" online after a windfall from a single marketing campaign, joint venture relationship, or product launch, for instance. Then they start blowing all their money on cars, clothes, trips, and whatever other expenses, instead of reinvesting it into their business.

Name the industry, and you'll find many of these people positioning themselves as coaches, consultants, or (my favorite) *thought* leaders! How about being a *results* leader instead?

Honesty is integral to a strong collaboration. If I'm looking to partner with someone, or hire an employee, and they're trying to position themselves as bigger, better, and bolder than they actually are: it's a disaster waiting to happen.

The best partners are humble, honest, and thoughtful people.

If you have found yourself over-embellishing your results, numbers, or experience, I say stop lying to yourself and others.

For any successful collaboration to take place, each person must be willing to lay their cards on the table and be honest about their assets. What skills do they bring to the table? Who's on their team? What's their cashflow like? How well do they know their competitors? Can they give me a clear idea of their strengths and weaknesses?

When like minds come together and strategize, new businesses can be born. Other times, each company can grow and benefit from each other. Sometimes there aren't really areas for collaborating directly, but perhaps either party can make a referral. Each week I look into approximately 15 businesses with the intention of either buying or partnering. Yet, if ever there is a hint the person is not being 100% honest, the interaction is over.

Be a Worker

No matter how successful you become, how much money you earn, or how much attention and praise you gain in your career; you must see yourself as a member of the ground crew. You are a member of the team.

You wake up every morning, put on your hardhat, your steel toe work boots, get your tool belt on, and go to work. You may be wearing a ten-thousand-dollar suit in a corner office and about to go speak in boardroom full of executives. But in your own mind you never lose a connection with that hard-labor mentality. You're always a ground worker. You never scoff at the idea of grabbing the shovel or pickaxe, and heading to work with the crew and putting in your time.

I did that with the mulching business. I got in those heavy machines and did the work with my crew. I had to know what it's like, speaking to the clients, hearing their concerns, and making sure the job was done right. I don't need to be there on the day-to-day. But if a challenge comes up, I can confidently address whatever it is. I have the full trust of my team because they know I'll do whatever it takes to get the job done.

People talk. They talk as if their words are real.

They talk about what they're going to do.

They talk about their dreams and ambitions.

They talk about their past achievements.

They talk, talk, and then talk some more.

That's the majority of people. Usually they're just talking themselves up. But when it comes to their work ethic, it doesn't take long for most of talkers to fizzle out and fade away.

The real winners focus on *doing.*

They get up early.

They get their job done.

If they're talking, it's about the job they got done.

Then, they're moving on to the next thing in silence.

If the job is not done, they get it done.

If their actions don't produce a result, they immediately pivot.

They correct themselves, shift, readjust, and implement.

Being an entrepreneur requires sacrifice and discipline. You've got to offset short-term pleasures in order to gain big future rewards. Your neighbor invited you to a cookout? Your friends want to go bowling? What about the big game, and spending this afternoon eating pizza, drinking beer, and goofing around with your pals? It takes a tremendous amount of fortitude to remain on your path.

You can only remain if you've set your path in the first place. So, don't feel bad about working while other people are sleeping. There's plenty of time for fun once you've achieved your goals.

Wear your work ethic like a badge of honor.

It's like a secret handshake into a club that only 1% of the population know exists, or are a part of.

Your work ethic also enables you to collaborate with other players who perform at your level.

That may be employees that you're hiring (which I'll get to in a moment), and it also may be partners you work with on new deals and opportunities.

Be a Collaborator

Did you know that two horses running in parallel don't create two horsepower? No. They actually create approximately. *three* horsepower. The combined effort of two horses increases the power of both. It's the same in business.

I mentioned in the introduction after I had scaled my own business, I started investing in other entrepreneurs. Sometimes it's through capital. Other times it's through joint ventures, equity partnerships, or consulting.

As you can probably guess, the number of businesses I look into is much larger than the number I end up investing in.

It's probably a 100/1 ratio.

Also, in order to do that effectively requires lots of thinking, time, energy, and due diligence. As a result, I collaborate with other experienced investors and entrepreneurs. We put our capital together, share resources, and we hustle in unison. Two horses: three horsepower.

Kyle is one of those business partners.

The first time I met Kyle, literally within the first 30 seconds, I walked into his office and he threw me a hardhat with his company logo on it, and in one breath said: "Michael, good to meet you, let's go make some pickups." and started walking out the door. Without missing a beat, I said, "Your car, or mine?"

We almost both started laughing right there, because we immediately understood each other. We didn't need lots of small talk to get acquainted. We let our work ethic do the talking for us.

Those are the type of collaborations you want to create: professionals who produce results.

My personality is different from Kyle's.

Kyle thinks fast, talks fast, and implements fast.

I think fast, talk slowly, and take my time to consider options to implement.

Yet, we are a one-hundred percent match in our work ethic and discipline.

If I have an idea, I'll text it to him, and he responds within a couple minutes.

5:30 AM? 3:36 PM? 9 o'clock?

Whatever time it is: when I text Kyle, those three little dots on my messenger start jumping up and down, showing that he's about to respond.

Both of our minds are wired for the constant hustle.

If something isn't working, we don't care who is right or wrong. We look for what's best for our business. We are both flexible and willing to pivot when needed.

We're constantly asking, "What did we miss? How can we sharpen this process? How can we add more value?"

When we're doing a deal, investing in a new business, or partnering with a company, we analyze each other's ideas and mindsets, searching for the best possible opportunity to raise the bar higher, raise our standard of performance, and disrupt our competitors.

Be a Leader

The following is a list, in no particular order of the qualities I've observed in good leaders. This is by no means a complete list. Yet, these are some of the qualities I remind myself of on a regular basis, as well as what I look for with our management team, partners, vendors, and employees.

Leaders keep a balance between creativity and analysis. Always be open to new ideas, but at the same time, test each new idea and gauge its performance objectively. That way, you're getting in the habit of analyzing the data to make an accurate judgement of whether each new idea is worth investing the organization's resources in. You must be open to new ideas and the positive change these may bring, but be cold about ending projects that aren't working. Embrace both positive and negative feedback however it shows up. Taking risks are the only way to get real feedback to base new actions on. Make sure you're constantly checking in with yourself, and making your future accomplishments excite you, and even make you feel a little nervous. But always know your numbers.

Maintain your vision. I've brought this up multiple times, and will stress it again in regard to your leadership capability. Leaders always have a personal vision of how they want to see the organization develop. We make sure every policy and proposal from any strategy session matches with that vision. We set tangible goals that are aligned with our vision. In other words, you're holding both the macro and micro targets in mind at the same time: always seeing the big picture, and maintaining the day to day course.

Eliminate conventional thinking. Any leader with a large enough vision *must* think outside the box. The statistics vary, but it's something like 5% of Americans have enough money to retire. That means 95% don't understand their finances. That also means that, 95% of the people you talk to in everyday life have zero idea about how to build a successful business, or become independently wealthy. Leaders know conventional is exactly that: conventional, ordinary, same-old-same-old. Everything "tried and true" is in the past. Why would any pathfinder rely on it, then, as a basis for their possibilities in life? What is possible can never exist in the past. It's only in the present and future. Conventional wisdom said: "it's impossible to run a mile in fewer than four minutes." Roger Bannister didn't listen. He would never have broken the record, running a mile in 3:59.4, if he accepted what was commonly accepted as fact.

Persevere through failure, *and success*. I've spoken to you about overcoming obstacles, and pivoting through challenges. But what about *persevering* through success? I have a warning for you. When you have paid your dues consistently and over enough time, at some point your actions are going to pay off. Again: causes and effects. Plant enough seeds in the right soil, take care of them with water and sunshine, and you will have plants. It's math. So, you've been performing the daily tasks, and finally all that effort has compounded into a large win. Perhaps it's a monthly revenue target, a new client, a major contract. Whatever it is, it's something you perceive as "making it to the big time." Certainly, it's a bigger accomplishment compared to anything you have personally experienced. That is a critical moment. For many ambitious people, that's when they begin compromising their work ethic. They rest on their laurels, get complacent, show up later, and leave earlier. They don't continue setting bigger goals. They stop reviewing progress, and stop asking themselves the big questions. As a result, their employees grow complacent. That results in a lack of customer service and therefore loyalty from their customer base. They start losing revenue, good employees, and vendors, which further compounds the complexity of their situation. At some point, they close up shop. And what was the source? Ironically, the source was that they *succeeded*. But instead of seeing that success as a critical step in an *evolution*, they saw it as an *end*. I've seen that happen countless times with all sorts of highly ambitious, smart, and talented people. Keep this in mind. Never allow your success go to your head. Persevere through success.

Take 100% Responsibility. Great leaders never play the blame game. As Harry S. Truman would have said, "The buck stops here." If they authorized a plan and it fails, a strong leader accepts full responsibility for the loss and immediately works on ways to not repeat the same procedure that resulted in loss. If my staff doesn't show up, or solve an important problem, that's *my* responsibility. It's yours, too, because you hired them and you trained them. If my team has a problem, I am their first line of defense. That is why I always know how to operate anything that is a part of my business. I could never be the first line of defense if I did not understand each role of the business completely. I train 90% of my support team myself. Perhaps at a larger scale that would not be possible. But when I'm scaling a business from 5 million in revenue to over the ten-million-dollar mark, that level of detail *is* possible. I do not absolve myself of any responsibility. My job is being a professional firefighter sometimes. I put out fires and see how my staff can fix things so that everyone gets a paycheck at the end of the week. I may even have to be a chameleon and change roles multiple times a day, still, depending on what's happening. To use a metaphor from baseball, I am a good cleanup hitter. My staff can always rely on me to be their power hitter. It is my role to hit the home runs and clean up all the bases for the team.

Create an All-Star Team

As a start-up, you're the first employee, and you can only do so much. You only have a certain amount of hours in the day.

If you're going to grow past your current plateau, you're going to need to clone yourself a few times by hiring assistants to take on tasks you've been doing. Otherwise, you'll continue maintaining the status quo and continue doing everything yourself.

In other words: outsource or stay stuck.

Since you have already created some level of success in your business, hire new employees or assistants who express the same level of enthusiasm for their job as you.

If you need an administrative assistant, hire someone who loves organizing people and things, someone who enjoys color-coding post-it notes and digital calendars and travel arrangements.

Since your assistants enjoy their job, you will have less stress having to double-check their work. This frees up your mind and energy for money-making tasks.

If you need bookkeeping help, then hire people who absolutely love numbers, people who take pride in their jobs and in their product, people who excel at those tasks.

This guarantees that they will put passion in their work and do a good job for you.

We have a few standard questions we always ask at our interviews…

- What do you think about your current job?
- What do you think about your profession?
- Why are you looking for a new job? (Are they looking because they don't like *who* they're working for, or *what* they do every day? (There's a big difference between the two).

Instead of hiring someone who just wants a job, I want to be selective and ask specific questions to get the answers and results I am looking for.

I know I can fix "I don't like who I am working for."

But I can't fix "I don't like what I do every day."

If you are not having fun every day, you must find something else to do. It's a long life. You have got to enjoy getting up every morning. If not, you are going to make everyone sick.

I was joking with a friend of mine that staffing an organization is like running a zoo, or a circus.

You know it feels that way sometimes!

The more I thought about it, the funnier it became, but also *true!*

Think of that movie, *Madagascar.*

At the beginning, before the plot thickens, a tiger, hippo, giraffe, and a zebra wake up in the morning and cannot wait to perform for the people who come into the zoo.

The people in the zoo have paid to be there.

They bought their ticket, and have high expectations.

That's like your clients and customers.

They've paid you to deliver on a promise.

Their expectations are high too.

The animals in the zoo are all unique.

The tigers are go-getters, like sales people.

The hippos are nurturing like the HR department.

The giraffes are smart like accountants.

What are the Zebras? You decide.

The analogy is less important than understanding this: you're putting on a show every day, and each player has a role to perform.

You hire a few ring leaders (managers) to manage the tigers, hippos, giraffes, zebras, and pandas (staff).

Together, the team puts on a show every day.

Each unit is interdependent.

You hire the managers who think like you (or as close to you as possible).

You take the time at the outset to outline your objectives.

I hire the best ringleaders.

The ringleaders make sure they hire the best zebras and hippos.

In this way, everyone is in accord and working on the same objectives, as defined by me.

You want people working with you who have a personal vision of themselves that is in alignment with you: building a great company that's doing big things. When those intentions line up, those people are the ones who know how to get a job done.

When I need something accomplished, I just lay it in their lap. Their job is to think out of the box and figure out a solution. If they need any help, they know they can pick up the phone and call me.

I would be glad to support them in any way at first. But they all must take a shot at solving their challenges independently.

One of the biggest lessons I've learned in the last two decades is not to buy companies or jobs: invest in *people*.

I invested in a concrete company and planned to use their operators.

It turned out to be a bad choice.

Their processes and machinery were some of the top in the industry.

But the people were not in alignment with the values I'm laying out here, and the deal turned into a disaster.

I personally meet with the entire staff so they can bring up anything that isn't working according to plan.

I meet separately with the managers who share any challenges they may be experiencing.

This way, everyone feels they are part of a team that is working toward a common objective, and everyone plays a vital role in the efficiency of the organization.

This is not lip service. I show my team I value them.

When they do a wonderful job, I make sure to give them premiums and gifts on a regular basis to award positive performance.

Likewise, because my staff show they are dedicated to our success, I experience very little employee turnover. Some of our staff have been with us for almost two decades, and I think some of them will never leave.

I encourage staff to train for new roles or re-purpose their current role and take it to a new level. They also value autonomy and complete ownership at work, along with the opportunity to grow with our companies.

When your staff are successful, they will go the extra mile to make your company successful. They work in a fulfilling environment and experience personal growth. In this way, everybody is happy, and everybody makes money.

A doctor's office, a real estate agent, a publisher or anyone working in the service industry can benefit from staff who are interdependent with each other. A physician needs his or her hands free to practice medicine. He or she needs to have competent staff who are committed to their roles. No one role is more important than the next.

A receptionist who is disrespectful to patients on the phone while setting up appointments will have the same effect as a nurse who doesn't wash her hands between patients, or a billing supervisor who is lax with billing.

Each role is dependent on the other, and everyone plays a part in the successful running of that office. Each staff position must make the owner look good and be perceived by their clients as the top choice for their unique service.

The professional is successful, and the staff enjoy the benefits of his or her success in the form of job security and tenure and premiums and gifts, where appropriate.

A dentist could provide free dental care to his or her staff members; a primary care doctor could provide free medical consultations to staff, etc.

The professional is dependent on staff to do their jobs well, while the staff are dependent on the professional for providing stable employment.

Competent and enthusiastic staff can keep you in business. We are successful today because our team works well together.

Make sure you stay in your own lane. When you're doing what you love in your business, you attract people who love what they do. It's a trickle-down, "do as I do," mentality, not "do as I say."

The people who are best at accounting do the accounting. The people who love sales: get out there and sell. The managers work hard to optimize, automate, and delegate. They perform at their best, because you're leading by example. Diversity is an important characteristic of a healthy company. We all have different strengths and weaknesses. Finding what those are creates the opportunity to collaborate. Sometimes, work can be tedious, but we are successful when we put our brains together and focus on our strengths. That is when we find our balance and figure out a game plan for what needs to get done.

Commit to Excellence

If you're going to do something, make it excellent.

I believe it's important to stay with a task till it is done *right*.

You know perfection is not possible.

Yet, striving for it *is.*

This commitment to excellence is now an integral part of all my businesses and we ingrain that into the culture of our companies as well.

Some of them have even carried this approach into their own businesses. That's actually one of the unique things that has happened with a few of our employees.

Since we encourage them to develop a personal vision and maintain high standards of excellence, they've gone on to become investors and start their own side businesses too.

When one of my staff bought his own restaurant, he was able to apply that same mentality there every day.

Actually, during a recent conversation, this employee told me: "When you go to a restaurant, and you order your favorite food, you want to get that food cooked in a certain way, so that it is perfect. Everybody walking in that door expects things to be done that way. When it's not done perfectly, you can lose customers. Delivering the same quality of customer experiences across our business is a critical daily mission, and I got that from working in your businesses."

I appreciated the compliment, but convey the story because that's the type of impact you can create in other people's lives by always outperforming your personal best. Whatever the record is: beat it. That's excellence!

Always Sell

As an entrepreneur, you are always selling.

When you're selling to a client or customer, you find out what their needs and desires are, and then communicate the benefits of your products and services to them.

When you're marketing, you're selling strangers on why they should get to know you. You're selling them on entering their contact information into your sales funnels, and selling them through your marketing materials on what makes you different from other vendors.

You sell to your employees when you're delegating. You're selling with vendors, partners, associates, and more.

One of the greatest assets you have is your ability to get your ideas into other people's heads, accept those ideas as something good for them, and compel them take action.

That's more valuable than money itself.

The words you use to do this are important. But what's more important is how well you listen. It's about the open-ended questions you ask – the *who, what, where,* and *why* – to establish what your prospects really desire, and how they explain their wants. When you do this, you're able to understand where your products or services match. And since you listened, you'll be able to explain that match using words your prospect uses.

Set Your Planning Time

Setting time in your calendar to do "deep thinking" will serve you well in your business. This doesn't have to be too cerebral. It can be as simple as asking yourself a series of meaningful questions:

- What has happened over the last x [amount of time] that I'm proud of? (reviewing the long-term past and rediscovering those moments where you were really "going for it.")

- What happened over the last month, both positive and negative?
- What do I want over the next 90 days, year, 3 years, etc.?
- What are our next steps?
- What can we stop doing that would produce leaps in progress?
- What are our biggest dangers that could prevent our goals from happening?
- Who are our best strategic partners or resources?

When I started my first business, I had an idea of where I wanted to be five years down the road based on my own personal motivation. At the time, I aspired to travel and experience other cultures.

It's important to first know your *why*; the real motivation for doing what you have set out to do. After you've figured out your *why* you can then figure out your *how*. Having a firm hold on your mission gives you the grit to stick to your objective. And those planning sessions are absolutely necessary for clarifying where you are, compared to those targets.

Envision what a three-year plan could look like. It's not set in stone. It's just an exercise. It's a way of stretching your imagination toward the long term.

Having a three-year plan in the tech support business is kind of insane because the industry changes so rapidly. Yet, the office you work from, the car you drive, the house you live in, the size of your team, the type of comments you hear from your team about their workplace, how you feel about your business – these can all be things to envision.

Proverbs 29:18 so wisely states, "Where there is no vision, the people perish." It's crazy doing business just for the sake of making money as an end. You must have a vision, a reason, a worthwhile goal, and some tangible means for getting there.

Set benchmarks every ninety days. That means, at the end of each quarter you take time to evaluate what went right, what went wrong, and how to tweak your progress to do better next time. Same with each month: take that time to review and reevaluate your plan to insure you are staying on course.

Nothing in life is set in stone. Situations are never stagnant. They are always fluid. Allow yourself to shift and pivot. If you have a firm plan for where you want to be, your method for getting there can change. Keep your finger on the pulse of your industry and continue to reevaluate progress and action every year, quarter, and month.

PART THREE: YOUR SYSTEMS

> **WANT TO MASTER THE SCALE-THEN-SELL SYSTEM?**
>
> Check Out the Complimentary Scale-Then-Sell Resources at:
>
> www.ScaleThenSell.com/Book

Not all time is created equally.

We can use our time on tasks that fuel us, or drain us. The difference between the two – fueled or drained – comes down to what you do, and when you do it.

In part two, we're going to look at how you can (literally) buy time and energy. You're going to do that by becoming great at creating systems, delegating, and outsourcing everything that drains you to someone who is energized by it.

Through my personal story, I hope you understand how outsourcing can change how fast you can scale your company.

Building a reliable team is <u>the</u> critical factor that gives any business a fighting chance to take over a market.

In the majority of cases, it's also the *only way* to create a company that manages itself.

A linear solo practice will almost always require personal labor to increase the bottom line or make any significant progress. By creating a team and systems, they're going to handle all those "how's" and remove that smoke screen from your vision, so you can keep taking massive action on your big-picture tasks (like going after more revenue).

I've heard other businesspeople complaining that, "employees are the worst part of any business! They want to take as much time off as possible, take as much money as possible, and put in as little work as possible!

They want equal money, but they don't want equal responsibility." I agree: the *wrong* employees do exactly that.

Yet, it is absolutely possible to find employees who find work meaningful. Those people are not only looking for a job; they're looking for belonging and being able to express their best work, be appreciated, and compensated.

When you set your mind on finding those types of people, they tend to appear. They'll do a great job because it is meaningful to them. They want to be part of a team because you're providing them with the resources to maximize their gifts and talents.

In this following section, I'm going to share with you delegation and automation insights that gave me the biggest "ah-ha" moments in my career up to this point.

I've done my best to omit clichés and run-of-the-mill productivity strategies you've probably heard a million times before. However, you'll notice what I share *is* basic. That's a good thing.

As you progress as an entrepreneur, you'll see the most effective people, as well as productive and profitable companies, are simply mastering the basics. Plants only need soil, sunshine, and water to produce fruits. Those are a plant's basics. In the same way; entrepreneurs need a market, systems, and the guts to go after their dreams.

Once we cover my biggest "ah-has," I'll give you a series of questions you can ask yourself to help you clarify which tasks you need to delegate *first*.

This will put you on a positive track going forward, and gain momentum. Remember: take these steps on a regular and ongoing basis. Follow them long enough so they become ingrained habits.

My hope for you is that you'll be able to get some of your *time* and *energy* back by paying for someone else's who is happy about the exchange.

Know what you want, then who can do it

In the introduction, I mentioned I'm a partner in a bakery. The baker knows how to bake delicious chocolate-chip cookies. They are really good too. She loves making them.

She could make chocolate-chip cookies all day long and never get tired of the process. It's a form of art to her.

I don't know how to make cookies. I only know how to eat them. I figure: let's keep it that way. She can make the cookies and I'll eat them while I systematize, automate, and delegate the processes in her bakery so we can increase her volume and profit by multiples.

I provide my team and infrastructure to our bakery partner. We come in and eliminate everything redundant, systematize and automate anything that can be, set up a new income model with higher profit margins, and incorporate our talented marketing and sales people and systems to increase the volume.

My bakery partner is now in the most creative position she's ever been in her life. What was once a painful chore to her, turned into a new business full of passion. She has regained her life back. She's making cookies, cakes, pastries, and making more money than she's ever made. Plus: our team is handling every task that used to drain her time and suck her energy. That's when one and one equals eleven.

We created the same outcome with the Amazon store. When I bought the business, it had just two employees. One of them was the owner. But I scaled this up to fourteen employees in two months. My first task was figuring out where the internal team had problems. I hired somebody to do what the current team didn't enjoy doing. The business soon went from one hundred clients to five hundred clients within the first two months.

These two stories are examples of personal visions connecting with one another to create an even bigger vision. But in order to create that successful partnership, and bring those two mutual visions to life, we had to clarify two things…

Roles and Results

Understanding roles and results is a major step to scaling your company.

A role is the "*who*." Who is producing a result?

The result is the "*what.*" What needs to get done?

It may sound like I'm overemphasizing these points, but it's important to understand, because the "*how*" is one of the things that causes business owners to stay small.

See, when you start your business, you have this idea of what you want to create. It's the big vision I mentioned earlier. You've got the direction in mind, and you're pursuing it. It feels productive.

You're making progress.

You're gaining momentum.

You're feeling hot, making sales, marketing your service, doing well. Then, at some point, you get stuck because you need to know *how to do* something.

- *How* do you set up that website?
- *How* do you figure out the ad manager?
- *How* do you configure the email server?
- *How* do you get a call-back number?
- *How* do you design a logo?
- *How* do you use accounting software?

All sorts of how's come into the picture, and they create a smokescreen over your personal vision. In the beginning, it doesn't feel like a big deal. Sure, you can figure out how to use that graphics program. Quickbooks? No problem. You can figure it out. Setting appointments? Why pay someone to do it for you… you can do it yourself and save the money, right? So, that's exactly what you do.

Bit by bit, you spend your time and energy on those how's. At some point, you max out your time. It's all used up. That's the self-employed rut: when every day feels like a hamster wheel. Again: not all time is created equally. The more time you spend on each of those how's, the less time you use growing your business.

With every *how*, there is an opportunity cost. Example: let's say, you want to earn $500/hour. You spend at least three hours in the day, doing jobs you could hire someone else to do for $25/hour. You may not realize it, but you're hiring yourself for those jobs. Plus: in many cases, you're doing the same job *in more time* than what someone else could do it in less. It takes me five times as long to write a sales letter as a professional copywriter, and they'd do a better job of it, faster.

The solution is to first determine *what* results need to get done. For instance: *scheduling meetings with clients*. You know exactly *how* to do this. You've done this so many times, it has become a habit. It's a straight-forward task that doesn't seem like it takes much of your time. Yet, that back-and-forth is eating your time, and certainly your mental energy.

Plus: it opens you up to answering questions about your client's other concerns or issues they may be experiencing.

So, you're ready to delegate that to an assistant. Great! What other results take time, drain your energy, and could be handed off to someone else? That's what you need to ask yourself. Simply compile a list of the key results you do that someone else could. For instance:

- Sending invoices
- Answering the phone
- Scheduling appointments
- Following up with existing clients, past clients, prospects, etc.
- Hosting a webinar

Now you've got your lists of results. Let's continue with the example of *scheduling meetings with clients*. You most likely have not organized the steps for scheduling a meeting with clients into a replicable form. You've just been *doing* it yourself. My guess is, also, that you do it differently each time (one of the reasons these tasks take so much energy). So, the next step is creating a document showing someone else how to successfully complete the task. That document is called a Standard Operating Procedure (SOP).

A SOP is basically a checklist; a step-by-step guide; an outline that shows exactly how to produce a result. Imagine if someone could watch you set appointments. They take notes of every single step from the beginning, middle, and end. Then, they teach the steps to someone else. That's what an SOP does. For scheduling meetings, an SOP may look like:

- Assistant schedules meeting with client.
- Send message (b) through social media, email, text, or phone call.
- "Hi [first name], I'm [assistant's name] contacting you on behalf of [your name] to schedule an appointment in regard to [purpose of meeting]. Would [date and time] work? Thank you! Sincerely, [assistant's name + contact].
- Confirm appointment is set with client.
- Assistant ensures [your name] calendar has all proper links for meeting.
- Prep notes are included with the calendar link to ensure [your name] knows the purpose of the meeting and ideal outcomes. (Is the call about Strategy? Review? Optimization?)

Again, you're creating these SOPs so you can transfer your current role to someone else. That person will be doing what you are currently doing.

That will free up your time so you can work on more valuable, revenue-producing activities. They'll be producing those other results, so you don't have to. This needs to be replicable. It needs to be a system you can depend on, that someone brand new can come in, understand, use, and be successful at. Otherwise, you'll end up with a new role: babysitter. Your assistants, employees, or contractors won't have a clear idea of exactly what to do in order to produce a result for you.

You are likely doing all sorts of these tasks right now. Each of those tasks is taking your energy. At some point, you'll have a manager whose role is creating SOPs for every part of your company. Until then, it's your objective to know *what* results you need done, what their importance is (*why*), define *who* needs to do them, and begin weaning yourself off the hamster wheel of "more doing." Imagine: you no longer need to know *how* to do every single technical part of your business. That doesn't mean you're going to sit back and drink martinis on a beach. It means you can place more conscious attention on your main role as leader.

Never Delegate Your Courage

I understand how challenging it is to start delegating and outsourcing. When I first started scaling my IT support business, there were some growing pains around letting go of tasks that had become habitual.

I mentioned how I was receptionist, CEO and janitor all in the same day. One of the hardest parts was giving up control and trusting other people to do the work I'd been doing on my own, even though that work could be done by almost anyone with a head on their shoulders. It was hard to let go of the common misconception that, *"If I want something done right, I have to do it myself."*

That is an employee's and self-employed mentality. That's looking at the whole grape, as opposed to a watermelon. The guy working a job, and the solo practitioner people often share that mindset with one another. I understood that if I wanted to turn into a true entrepreneur, one who can scale and dominate the financial potential of my market, I had to think instead, *"If I want something done right: someone capable, talented, and reliable must do it."*

Then: take action toward finding those competent people, which requires courage.

Never Delegate Your Learning Curve

Aside from the courage and the mindset shift, it also took enduring the growing pains of a few bad hires. If you recall when you first started your business, there was probably a list of things you had no idea about.

Now, they're automatic behaviors you don't have to think about. You've already gained habits over your career, and delegating is simply a new one you're going to take on. With this new skill set comes a whole new learning curve. No matter how many books you read, audios you listen to, or videos you watch; at some point the rubber meets the road and you're going to be faced with learning opportunities that come from sour experiences.

Just Do It

Let's say you're ready to execute. You've prepared yourself mentally for the potential learning curve outsourcing and delegating presents to you.

Imagine a new possibility for your business and career.

Imagine showing up to workdays and doing *only the things you love* in your business. Imagine too, if your company could grow in those conditions, even if you're not physically there.

You maintain your company's vision.

You are in charge of the direction.

You focus on growth, innovation, and the big picture.

Yet, you're not caught in the weeds, pressing all the buttons, doing anything with *Excel* (unless you love it), or reading all those spam messages that came through your website's contact form.

Really imagine that for a moment. How would it feel to use your time only doing the things that *motivate*, *inspire*, and *energize* you on a regular basis?

Great.

Now, the reality of your situation is probably much different. I'm guessing a big percentage of your time is caught in the weeds pressing all those buttons I mentioned. This is not ideal for growth.

On my journey, aside from taking the leap of faith (the courage to act and start outsourcing), the second hardest part was defining exactly which tasks to outsource first, and then answering the question: "who should do those tasks?"

- What **drains** your energy in your business?
- What **distracts** you and takes you away from what you love?
- What **frustrates** you most?

- What is tedious, monotonous, or **boring**?

In his book *The Seven Habits of Highly Effective People*, Steven Covey first touched on the "Big Rocks" analogy as a tool for time management. If you had a jar to be filled with big rocks, pebbles and water, how would you do it?

The obvious answer would be to put the rocks, followed by the pebbles, and then the water into the jar. Now, imagine if the big rocks were your most important life priorities. If you don't put them into the jar first, you would never get them in at all.

So, don't let the pebbles and the water fill your life. Prioritize the big rocks instead. As Steven Covey says, "The key is not to prioritize what's on your schedule, but to schedule your priorities."

One approach to doing this is to use Dan Sullivan's Time System Entrepreneurial Time Management System. His planning system thinks of your time in terms of three different categories:

1. Focus days
2. Buffer days
3. Free days

While on Focus days 80% of your time is devoted to activities impacting your bottom line, Buffer days are for smaller tasks like email or accounting. But Free days mean a complete break from any work-related activity. All weekends are recommended as Free days. Ideally, an entrepreneur's planning system should include a combination of Focus days, Buffer days, and Free days. With the Buffer days and Free days acting as the real launching pad for the Focus days.

The disciplined pursuit of more with less is also the theme of the New York Times bestseller *Essentialism* by Greg McKeown. The book shifts the needle from doing more in less time to getting the right things done. Greg McKeown writes, "Essentialism is not about how to get more things done; it's about how to get the right things done. It doesn't mean just doing less for the sake of less either. It is about making the wisest possible investment of your time and energy in order to operate at our highest point of contribution by doing only what is essential."

That is an important transition in management thinking.

It is a shift from doing *more* to doing the *essential*.

CONCLUSION

What shapes the character of a real champion?

The most successful business people I have learned from, partnered with, been mentored by, or personally mentor have certain characteristics.

Almost invariably they wake up early, stay late, and work harder and smarter than their competitors.

They put in consistent, focused work, day in and day out.

They do this over the long term.

There is no substitute for putting in your time: grinding, over delivering, and out maneuvering.

I'll say it one last time: change like that <u>never</u> happens overnight.

It takes everything you've got.

It takes all your courage, all your determination, all your stamina and emotion.

Everything.

If you really want to scale your company, here's what your calendar is going to look like…

WEEKLY SCHEDULE

RISE AND GRIND 24/7
NEW WEEK, NEW GOALS!

MONDAY	**HUSTLE**
TUESDAY	**HUSTLE**
WEDNESDAY	**HUSTLE**
THURSDAY	**HUSTLE**
FRIDAY	**HUSTLE**
SATURDAY	**HUSTLE**
SUNDAY	**HUSTLE**

* You can't have a million dollar dream with a minimum wage work ethic

That's my personal calendar.

If it's yours too, you are going to enjoy a very rewarding life as an entrepreneur.

Thank you for reading *Scale Then Sell*.

If you're ready to scale your company If you are a talented, motivated, and ambitious entrepreneur with a great idea or business model that is currently working – yet, <u>you've reached a plateau</u> in the progress you're able to make on your own: I am interested in hearing about your model, and potentially investing in you. Whether that means a new injection of capital that increases your capacity to market or hiring more staff, or it means utilizing our businesses infrastructure (a relentless team of skilled market-makers and systems experts), I am willing to hear what you have to offer, and discover if we could collaborate together.

I hope to see you in an upcoming training, or within our community of ambitious entrepreneurs.

Sincerely,

Michael Byars

About the Author

Michael Byars is a former "one-man company" turned serial entrepreneur. Whether you're learning how to lead and delegate; raise growth capital; position your company to sell, or seeking a strategic partner to grow your business, this book is a bible to get you to the finish line.

Exiting your business is a process. The principles you learn will enable you to implement key strategies to rapidly drive cash flow, improve the bottom line, and create a multiplying-effect when you exit the professional way.

Go to www.ScaleThenSell.Com/Book for additional bonuses that come with *Scale Then Sell*.

www.ingramcontent.com/pod-product-compliance
Lightning Source LLC
Chambersburg PA
CBHW070301220526
45465CB00004B/1689